Wait in the Stillness

Poems of Loving God and Others

By Don MacLeod

Bound & Determined
Minneapolis

Wait in the Stillness

Copyright © 2014-2017 Don MacLeod

All rights reserved under the Berne Convention

No part of this publication may be reproduced, distributed, or transmitted in any form or by any means, including photocopying, recording, or other electronic or mechanical methods, without the prior written permission of the publisher, except in the case of brief quotations embodied in critical reviews and certain other noncommercial uses permitted by copyright law.

For permission requests, write to the publisher at:
"Attention: Permissions Coordinator"
Bound & Determined
2637 27th Ave. S.
Suite 219
Minneapolis, MN 55406

Or email bound.determined@gmail.com

First Bound & Determined Edition

ISBN 978-1-947261-04-4

Library of Congress Control Number: 2017908011

Dedication

To Ellen Finholt MacLeod
It's not the same since you left, but would I feel so deeply if you had stayed?

Table of Contents

Open Your Heart
Silence of the Stars
The Darkness Falls
The Dark Moon
Ecstasy
The Journey Home
Immortal
I Heard the Loneliness Call My Name
I Can't Tell You
Wait in the Stillness
My World
I Saw My Heart
We Hold Our Hearts Out
I Want To Touch God So Deeply
The Cost of Peace
The Valley of the Immortal
He Got Up
Can I Talk To You
I Tried To Help A Blind Man See
When We Are At Peace

Why You Are Alive

My God

That Face

The Gray Thief

We Are Creeping Out of the Darkness

Despair

In My Mind

How Do I Explain

To Julie Z

Intelligence

Absence

Dawn

Can You Move With the Universe?

Broken toys

Lovely

I'm Going To Shave Your Head?

So Many Ideas

So Many Things to Say

I Can't Tell You

Secret Lover

It Smelled Like

Breath

Sometimes

I Saw My Heart

Thank God it's Saturday

There Was a Man

Where Has the Will Gone

Wandering Soul

The Vulnerability of the Heart

Nothing Is Easier

Acknowledgements

Open Your Heart

Open your heart
Don't just read this
Open your heart and let love in
Open your heart and let love out
Don't hold back
Give and give and give
Receive and receive and receive
No one should ever have to earn our love
Love is not a commodity to be bought and sold
Give it away like you have an infinite Supply
Because you do
You can never run out of love
Yet we squander it like there's not enough to go around
As if we won't get it back
In my experience, the more you give, the more you get
It takes practice though
If you don't learn to receive, how will you get it back

Silence of the Stars

I listened to the silence of the stars rushing by
They called my name in whispers so loud
So loud
I thought my heart would explode
So quiet
Only I heard them call
My heart did answer to their whispers
It did explode, as it sang their song
It sang in harmony
It sang as loud
It sang the joy of the night sky wide open
It grasped the quiet melody and shook it out
Cobwebs and all
From it fell, a very small, very quiet…
Well, you know

The Darkness Falls

The darkness falls and it seems there is no way out.
No one understands the blindness that has fallen on me.
I am in a hole that I can not find my way out of.
I am told the way out is in front of me, take a step, but I can't see even a little in front of me.
The darkness has fallen and I am trapped, the dark thoughts have surrounded me, there is no way out.
The darkness falls again and the hole seems deeper.
The way out more obscured.
There is no hope to find the way out.
The light is only a shadow of memory, the darkness is everything.
The earth is caving in, closing in and the hole is getting tighter.
Breathing is getting more difficult.
Fear is now my loudest companion.
God cannot hear my pleas as the walls grow thicker and the hole digs itself deeper.
My life is becoming a whisper.
The angels can't reach me.
There is no rope long enough.
I grasp the walls of the hole to not fall deeper, but it knows all I want to do is let go.
I am tired of the fight, I want to succumb and let the walls collapse, but something won't let that happen.
I beg for the wall to collapse and allow the darkness to take me, but something won't let that happen.
Something is lifting me.

Something is filling the hole.
Something is breaking the darkness.
Something will not allow the hole to swallow me.
Somewhere something is pushing me up and out and it hurts.
Oh it hurts and I still want the darkness to swallow me.
I have no fight, I want the pain to stop, I want the hole to take me.
I am being lifted, I am being raised up.
I can feel the hole's power diminishing.
The pain is diminishing.
The darkness is diminishing.
I am lying on the ground and a faint light, a very faint light is surrounding me.
My desire for the hole is diminishing.
My fear is diminishing.
My pain is diminishing.
The light is stronger and I can see there is no hole now, never was.
The light is stronger and I can see the darkness is losing its power
The light is stronger and I can stand now.

The Dark Moon

The Dark Moon enjoined us to stay

Our hearts would not let us

The Dark Moon said
O see what I can show
A power not seen before

Our hearts pulled us to flee

A power that will make you great and beloved
A power that will make all worship you

Our hearts tugged harder to get us away
Our ears wanted to hear more

A life awaits of more than you can imagine
A glory where you will be king or queen
All the wonders you could ever want at your feet

Our hearts panicked beating faster
Our lust begging us to listen, begging to be fed

No one will ever betray you
All will have to worship your greatness
You can do anything you wish

Our hearts said NO

Our hearts said LIES
Our hearts said ENOUGH
Our hearts stood firm and said
Power is not love
Power is not fulfilling
Our ears wanted more
Power creates a vacuum in the heart that will never be filled
Power kills
Power destroys
We stepped away

The Dark Moon gasped

Only love can give you what you truly want
Only love can fill the gaps in your heart

The Dark Moon spit

The real wonders lie in the true love that sits deep within

The Dark Moon shattered and fell to dust

Our hearts grew strong and we continued on

Ecstasy

Ecstasy is not a word we hear often
It is not something that is normal for us as a human living now
It's not a word we understand
It is really not a word that can be understood
Either you have felt it
Or you haven't
Some think of sexual ecstasy, but no, that is not true ecstasy
Ecstasy is when you have allowed the Divine into you
Ecstasy is when there is nothing but the Divine in you
It can last a second
It can last an eternity
That moment when it hits, when it touches you, YOU
The real You
You no longer exist
You are no longer
Then the moment it withdraws, that moment is when you are you again

That moment and only in that moment are you really aware of this Divine ecstasy
As it is gone
But, you can dive back in
You can lose yourself
You can be one, over and over and over again with that moment
Like an addict, it will call you
It will bring you back eventually
Your heart will not allow you to stay away
Your soul will not allow you to stay away
Your entire being can not be without drifting into it once more
The peace calls like nothing else
The joy of it calls like nothing else
The absolute being of it is like nothing else

The Journey Home

I stood on the beach
I was maybe three
I felt this something
This Something
I could not describe it
But it was there
Like hunger
Like thirst
A primal need
It was all around me
It was huge
This Want
This Desire
It was inside me
But for what
Nothing in This world
Where
Even though my family was close by
I was lost
Alone
But I had found something
I had found something big
I was three

Immortal

I may be immortal, but you are the one that will live forever
You have Touched my heart and will be there throughout eternity

I Heard the Loneliness Call My Name

I heard the loneliness call my name
I asked what it wanted
It called me
I said no
It called again whispering my name so lovingly
I could not resist this time
I followed it
It took me deep
It took me where I didn't want to go
Or so I thought
We got to the bottom and I saw
This was MY call
Me calling
Me calling to my Creator to come to me
My Creator answered and said
I am already here
I said
What is this loneliness
The answer was clear
My call to be one with my Creator
That deep desire that wants to know no separation
It was clear
This is what we come here for
It's where we can be separate enough to know
To know the feeling of desire so strong that we will do anything to appease it
That we will even eventually give up everything to be one with it

To stand here/there as a finite being
To stand there risking being destroyed to touch the infinite for an ever so brief moment
A moment that can fulfill a lifetime with ecstasy
A moment that will destroy your life
A moment that will fill you up completely
A moment that is worth giving up everything, everything, everything

I Can't Tell You

I can't tell you how deeply I feel connected to God
I can't tell you because there are no words to describe it
I can't tell you because you wouldn't believe me
People alive today don't connect to God
People alive today don't experience God
If they do, they are crazy
Point taken
But I connect
I see the infinite
I have touched it
It has touched back
Some people think you have to die to do that
Or come close
I did as a baby
Came close
I know it changed me
I know it made me know that we are not alone in this world
I know it made me know that God never went away
I know

Wait in the Stillness

Wait in the stillness
Listen
Watch deep inside
There is a Universe that waits to be explored
Every speck of it made to fulfill your being
Beyond the comprehension of the human mind
But completely understood by the heart
No doubt
There we can dance with the Gods
They wait
They want to play
They revel in every discovery
Treasuring each moment of joy
You are their child
They have waited for so long for you to come
The have waited moments for you to wake up
Time doesn't exist and you have always been there
But not as well
Each moment you spend with them is great joy
Each moment is more than you can bear
Each moment destroys who you are
But rebuilds who you were and will become
Life is not normal there in the stillness
In the deep
Life is more than can ever be said

My World

My world
Is not your world
My world is a world of colors
That taste and have sound
My world is a world of feeling
That has colors and light
I'm inviting you to this world
But you say
You say nothing
You don't know it's an invitation
You can't see that it's an invitation
You fear the cost
You should
It will cost you everything
Everything
Nothing you think will be the same
Nothing you see will be the same
Nothing you believe will be the same
You will no longer believe
You can't
Because you will know
You will have to leave everything behind
Your old thoughts
Your old fears
Your old doubts
They are precious without question
As I said
The cost is dear
It will cost you everything

You will pay with your doubts
You will pay with your loneliness
You will pay with your anger
You will pay
Everything you have must be left behind
Everything you want must be left behind
Everything you need will be left behind
You will care when you let it all go
You won't care when it's all gone
You will taste the colors that are Divine
You will see the sound that pierces the illusion
You will know you are one with everything
I'm inviting you
To wake in a different world and taste the music so sweet
And dance in the moonlight of a thousand suns

I Saw My Heart

I saw my heart
It launched joy and peace to the world
It blew kisses to small children and dogs
It danced in the wind as the leaves swirled by
It sang the song of joy that plays deep within
It felt the sorrow of love that was lost
It embraced the Grace that comes with each breath
It holds the Mother Earth tightly and loves Her deep

We Hold Our Hearts Out

We hold our hearts out
We hope for a miracle every day
We pray that God is there
Not gone away
Disappointment falls over us when it doesn't come
Our hearts sink and weep
As our God is not there to hear us
But we are ignorant of that one miracle that happens every breath
The life coming and going as the air comes into the lungs and goes out
Each a moment where God has given us a gift unnoticed
And yet we pray and weep in our despair
The infinite coming and going every few seconds
Life
We don't even recognize it as the greatest miracle
We don't even see the preciousness of it until we are close to losing it
Some people would do anything in those last moments for one more
And we throw them away
Unnoticed
And we pray and weep for miracles every day

I Want To Touch God So Deeply

I want to touch God so deeply
I want to feel God so deeply
I want to know God so deeply
It's not an idle request
It's not something I read in a book
It comes from somewhere so deep in my being that
I can not even describe to you
It comes from the other side of the Universe
The internal, infinite Universe
That longing
That desire
To see the face of God and to touch it
And to be touched back
To know that God is real
But
You see
I know God is real
I have touched the face of God
I have been touched back
That's what is hard
Once is not enough
Once only makes you want more
Once makes you feel the separation deeper than you
felt before
Once makes the desire even stronger
The only way to do it
To be touched
Is to stay alive as long as possible
To be here

To be separate
To come to that moment when it happens again
And then it's not enough
And you want to live one thousand years so you can do it once again and again and again
Once more

The Cost of Peace

What is the cost of peace
It is the most expensive thing you can buy
The cost is your running thoughts
The cost is your things
The cost is the thises and the thats
The value is immeasurable
Do you know that
Have you felt peace that strong
Do you understand that peace is that valuable
That you should give up everything for it
Do you

The Valley of the Immortal

The Valley of the Immortal lies not in this world
It lies deep within our being
It lies in a place so silent
You can barely hear a heartbeat
It lies in the depths of darkness
But shines brighter than the sun
Oh your eyes can behold it
Closed tightly seeing only the one
The brightness of the Valley will pull you in
If you let it
If will feed you
If you let it
It will give you everything you never knew you wanted or needed
If you let it
It is so very hard to let it
We are taught not to let it
We are taught to guard our hearts
We are taught that love is fleeting
We know it is
But now
We are wrong
In the Valley of the Immortal
There are no lies or deceit
There is no room
There is no need
Your heart is naked and exposed
Your life is as it is
Acceptance is complete

He Got Up

He got up in his fear and anger
He knew they would not go
They wore him down like a grindstone
Stealing every ounce of energy
He did not give in to them though
He stood fast even when they promised
Promised him so much
To look after him
To protect him
To save him
From what
Only from himself
Only from who he could have been
Only from his dreams
Don't go there
They would say
Fearfully or angrily
Wise he thought
Tiring he thought
Best be safe they all agreed
Now he is bound so tight he can barely move
The constrictions are set
A light burns though
Deep within
Barely alive
But still burning
He looks when he can
But they catch him
He looks away

But he remembers
Barely
What if
He thinks
Be afraid
Maybe
It will make you angry
It might
There is only fear
The light is there though
It always has been
It feels good
It does not preach anger and fear
What if he fed it instead
Foolish they say
But what if
As he stares into the light

Can I Talk To You

Can I talk to you
There are so many things to say
Really there is only one thing to say
The rest can wait
Or doesn't really matter
What does matter is you are alive
No matter how awful things are
You are being given a gift
It makes no sense I know
Your life sucks and I'm telling you it's a gift
Let me tell you why
No
I will try to explain
I barely understand this myself
It is the most incredible secret ever
And I'm just telling you
That breath you just took and gave back
Where did it come from
Why did you get it
Not the air
The breath
That thing that without a thought
Keeps coming and going in us all
Who or what gives it
Find that answer
You will be wealthy beyond your imagination
Oh wait
I didn't tell you did I
Come closer

There is this place inside
This place where your breath comes from
A place that pulls each one in
And then lets it go
This place is calling you
You feel it
You know it's there
The door is always open
A universe waiting for you to jump in
Always calling
That's why you feel discontent
You can't ignore it
Well
You can
That is why you feel discontent
Ride the breath to this rendezvous
Fulfill yourself beyond your imagination

I Tried To Help A Blind Man See

I tried to help a blind man see
It was impossible
Not that he was truly blind
It was he didn't want to see
He didn't want to see the truth
The lies he knew were safer
The lies he held were familiar
The facts were too foreign for his mind
His belief mattered more
His belief was what was true
His belief held his world together
I thought no wonder you can't see
You would lose the world you hold so tight to
I questioned my own blindness
What do I not see because I am holding on
Am I willing to let my world collapse to see

When We Are At Peace

When we are at peace
This world is like a wind blowing in our face
Staying at peace takes effort
All the distractions blowing past as we walk through this world
Pulling at the fibers of our being
Distracting us from knowing God
Keeping us from our true self
There is another wind that blows
The breath
It comes
It goes
Each a blessing
Each a gift
That wind keeps us connected
That wind is our compass

Why You Are Alive

People think that there is something better than here
That heaven is better than here
That somehow it is a mistake for us to be alive
Why don't we see the gift that life is
What is it in us that doesn't recognize the preciousness of a human life
We think it's OK to shoot someone or kill them
Not all of us
No
What is it in human nature that fights so hard to stay alive yet can't see exactly why
If the afterlife is better
Why put us here
Why don't we just stay there
Why even come into human form
This is what we need to understand
Isn't there something incredible here
That we would be given the time here
And we do everything possible to stay here as long as we can
We fight so hard to stay here
Why
When heaven waits
Every living thing fights for life to the last second
I know and have met people that can't wait to die and go to Heaven
I feel really sad for them
I knew people that would give anything for more time here

I know people doing everything possible to stay here longer
I know living in this world can be a struggle
It doesn't matter
It's all an incredible gift we need to understand
Where inside is that thing that fights
Where is that little voice that says do everything you can do stay alive
Find that place
Sit there
Listen
Hear the story of why you are alive

My God

My God
Your God
Is there a God
What does God look like
Does God look like
I know
I don't think
I don't believe
I KNOW God is there
God is HERE
But God is not what YOU think
Or I think
Or believe
There is the problem
Believe
Belief is not knowing
Having FAITH is not knowing
Reading a book and memorizing it
Is NOT KNOWING
Knowing
Is experiencing

That Face

That face
The look of wonder on a child's face is so incredible
We all need to see the world this way
As there is so much we don't see
Because we think we know so much
And know what we see
What if we could live every day like this
Like we never saw it before
We haven't
Do you realize you have never seen this day before
It's brand new
Yet you/I treat it like it's the same old thing
Just like it was yesterday
What would happen if we hopped out of bed
Expecting it to be a new day
A different day
I'm willing to try

The Gray Thief

The gray thief has come again today
The gray thief takes from what little light we have
The gray thief removes the shadows from the earth
The gray thief washes the light from the trees
The gray thief removes the brightness from the snow
The gray thief takes without thought
The gray thief takes without compassion
The gray thief blows in with no sense of the longing that has been created
Our bodies crave the light
Our bodies crave the color
Our bodies crave the brightness of the world
Our hearts try to shield us from the gray
Our hearts try to see the light
Our hearts try to see the color
Our eyes want to swim in the beauty of color
Our eyes want the tickling of the shadow at the corner of our eyes
Our eyes want to embrace the shifting light through the trees
But the gray is all encompassing
Gripping our hearts with solemnness
Pulling us into it and trying to embrace us
Pushing any thoughts of sunshine and light away
It is not evil
It knows no better
The gray thief has come again today

We Are Creeping Out of the Darkness

The shortest day is behind us
The coldest nights are yet to come
The frost will creep slowly deeper into the ground
Our eyes will weep from the cold wind
Our bodies will beg for an early spring
The sun will shine brighter every day
The sun will shine longer every day
Reaching out to us giving hope of that longed for spring

Those silent things underfoot
Retreat in wait for warmer days

Our minds will be bleary from freezing
The freezing mind gets old

Despair

Despair sometimes you're my only friend
Walk with me
Tell me you love me
Hold my hand
Caress me that special way that only you can

Poverty of the Heart

I have seen so much poverty in my life, the poverty where people are lacking possessions, water and food. I have been thinking about top 1% of people in this country and how heartless some of them are. That's when it hit me what real poverty is. These people can have anything they want, but they have the poverty of generosity in their hearts. They have the poverty of sharing. They have the poverty of greed.

It made me realize that poor people are so much richer. I have seen a man with $10 give $1 to someone that had nothing. Who is richer? Who is really experiencing poverty, the worst poverty? It's not the man with $10.

Now I am hoping I can forgive those that live in the worst poverty of all now that I understand them better.

How small your world must be with little love or compassion for people less fortunate. Not reaching out to allow more love and people into your lives is very sad.

In My Mind

In my mind
I have fought the Ring Wraiths
I have battled Darth Vader and won
I have fought a war with arthritis and lost
I have battled depression and won
I have faced numbness and the battle goes on
There is a war raging in my spine
I am losing the battle to stiffness
But not the war
I am winning the battle against anger
I am losing the battle to love
Thank goodness
Peace is winning in my heart
The battle for loneliness is gone.
The battle for memory is slipping away
The war for joy is almost done
My body is a battlefield
My mind is a playground
My heart is winning my very soul from all

How Do I Explain

How do I explain the magnificence that is opening up inside? A freedom that I knew was there and hoped would come, but feared it wouldn't. It is here. It is now.

The capacity for love is in question. Can we absorb an infinite amount of love? Can we physically accept it? Can we mentally accept it? The capacity for love is said to be infinite, but that would mean we would have to become infinite. Becoming infinite is not an easy task.

Something is happening and I want to share it. I want the world to feel it. I want to feel it. Some part of me seems to think I have to share it first, wanting affirmation that it is true that it is real. The old doubtmaker itself rises up even in the greatest of ecstasy and asks if you are sure you feel that? That's its job and yes I am so sure I feel that. I am more sure of it than I ever have been. I am more sure of it than anything I have ever been sure of before. I want to let it embrace me even more. To take me deeper and further than my mind, my brain thinks is possible.

To Julie Z

I'm sorry for your loss. I hate that this is one more thing in your life that you don't need right now. It is a lot. People will say that God doesn't give you more than you can handle, but life does sometimes. It has nothing to do with God.
Getting broken down, can make us so vulnerable to the world. That is OK, we should be more vulnerable. It allows more love into our beings and we learn to not tolerate the things that don't promote or make love grow. That is the benefit.
I am sorry your heart hurts so much now. It will get better. It may not heal completely, but it will get better. The scars stay to remind us of the people we were and who we no longer want to be.
Let love comfort you in these days.

Intelligence

I used to think I was pretty smart. Then one day I realized I was more like Forest, Forest Gump.

Absence

Absence
Vacancy
Void
Lack
Empty
Opening

When the person you loved so dearly and lived with for 29 years leaves the planet, it leaves a space in you. A space that is hard to describe. Some people feel their total absence, but I am fortunate that I don't. I still feel her presence. Sometimes it was so strong I used to turn and see if she was there. So strong that I could hear her standing there, so strong that if I turned fast enough, I could have touched her. But no, she is gone. Her body is dust now. I saw her body when she had left it behind. I knew it wasn't her. I knew that it was the shell she had occupied for all those years, but it was not her. What was her, still existed, still thrived, still lived?

It was hard to mourn with her still here, but it was hard not to mourn with her so not here. The absence of her physical being is odd. The presence of her spirit is so comforting. We talk, rather, I talk, she communicates. Feelings mostly that I try to translate into words to try to get a better understanding. I know I'm missing things. She says it doesn't matter. That I'm clear enough.

There is so much we don't understand here. There is so much that we think that is so important. Stuff. It has no meaning. Work, unless it's our heart's desire, has no meaning. Things don't mean anything. Where we live means nothing. How we live means everything.

Ellen said from the other side, "Do everything, everything, everything possible to stay there.
Stay there as long as you can. Do everything, anything possible to stay in your body as long as you can. Accept everything even the pain. You have no idea."

I'm starting to have an idea.

Dawn

This is my friend Dawn
She runs through the world naked and screaming
She dares you to look and say something
But you can't
She doesn't want to be so vulnerable
But she can't help it
She doesn't want to be so loud
But it's who she is.
She can't help it
She is not normal
She can't be normal
It's not in her genes
It's not in her soul
It is nowhere in her being
She is here to change the world
She's learning to leave the desire for normal behind
Even though it still tugs at her
It calls to her telling her she will be more comfortable
She knows it's a lie
Her discomfort is from breaking free
Learning to fly on wings that aren't quite strong enough to hold her yet
Her discomfort is not knowing if they will truly hold her
Her discomfort is not knowing she can really let go and be herself
Her discomfort is not knowing how much she is truly loved

Falling in love was a struggle
Allowing herself to be loved was not easy
Being loved seemed like a trap
Being loved seemed confining
Being loved seemed like an end
She allowed this man to take her heart
She allowed this man to show her that he wanted to set her free
She allowed this man to love her and give her his heart
She allowed this man to set her free

Can You Move With the Universe?

Can you move with the Universe?
Can it feel the sway of your arms as you sweep them across the sky?
Can it feel the beauty of your heart as it moves you across the field of stars?
Does it feel the arch of your back as you bend backwards over the moon and reach for the ocean?
Is the silence flowing between you solid and unbroken?
Do your eyes penetrate the great darkness to become part of the lit Universe?
Do you drink it in?
Does the darkness pull at the deep fears that you hid deep within the strands of your being?

Broken toys

Some think broken toys are sad, but I look at them and think about how loved they are. I see kids with toys that are falling apart and the parents will tell you that they will not part with them for anything, because it is their favorite. First true loves. Eventually though, they do let go and those toys do get set aside. Still, the love remains.

I love to see people find old toys they had. Same reaction. OH I haven't seen this in so long. I took it everywhere. The love abounds, the smiles are huge and the memories take over and flash across the brows. I don't want to interrupt the moments when they happen. They are precious, but somehow, we say, it's just toy. Not really, they were a first true love.

Lovely

Life is lovely
Being in this world can be so hard sometimes, but life itself is incredibly lovely
The breath comes and goes as an unseen miracle every few seconds
The moments that I notice, my gratitude is overwhelming

I'm Going To Shave Your Head?

"OK, it's time. I'm tired of the clumps of hair falling out, I want you to shave my head."
"I'm going to shave your head?"
"Yep, let's go for it."
My heart was breaking in a way. I really didn't want to cut off all those beautiful long blond hairs, but she was so perky about it, I had no choice to join in. I wasn't going to be a Debby Downer. The chemo was hard enough, she didn't need me to be sad about this and for some reason, she was so happy about it. We went in the bathroom and I took the clippers and went over her head. We had draped a large yellow beach towel over her to catch the hair.
When I was done, she looked in the mirror and then smiled at me with her big beautiful smile. I looked at her and all I could see was Gandhi, with her round glasses, white pants and shirt and the towel draped around her shoulders.
I have a picture.

So Many Ideas

We have so many ideas of what it would mean to speak with God or be in God's presence. What if it was just a sweet moment connecting with the creator and that's all it was? Seas didn't part, bushes didn't burn and water didn't turn to wine. Would it still be a miracle? Would we let it be a miracle?

So Many Things to Say

There are so many things that I want to say.
There is nothing I can say.
The Silence says everything.
Total, absolute quiet inside is one of the loudest things I know.
How can I say what that Silence says so much better?
How can I convey what that Silence portrays so much better?
I can't.
We will let the Silence speak for itself then.

I Can't Tell You

I can't tell you some things I want to. I want to tell them, but they are to secret too share. Ok I will tell one. One big one. Inside is this space. This infinite space that is easy to access, but you have to know the secret key to see the path to it.

In that infinite space is more than the human mouth can describe. In fact, the human mouth can not put words to what is seen, heard, tasted, or felt there. It is beyond description.

Secret Lover

I have a secret lover.
You do too.
Every breath you take and give
That secret lover comes and goes.
Each breath is a kiss keeping you alive.
That secret lover breathing you so you can be in this world.
Thank that secret lover.
Be aware of that secret lover.

It Smelled Like

It smelled like heaven
Well
What I thought heaven would smell like
Intoxicating anyway
You walk into this tunnel
This odor touches your nose
Moves through your sinuses
Into your mouth
It doesn't just smell
It consumes you
All you want to know is
What the hell it is
You know you will never find out
The way you are walking is a sacred silent path
No one speaks on this path
No questions asked
But many answers lying at the apex of the tunnel
You arrive there
So much is in your heart you don't know
All you can do is be grateful you found the tunnel
You were allowed to enter
You pass the apex
Look back
Say thank you
Your heart is full
You receive the biggest smile in your life
It's plastered on your face.

Breath

There is this thing called breath
None of us seem to know what it really is
We take each one
We let them go
Like they are nothing
Like they are common
They are
Until they get fewer
Or hard to take
Then
Then they are not so common
Then they take on quite a bit of significance
They mean everything
Nothing else matters
But when they're easy to take again
They don't matter so much anymore
Why is tha

Sometimes

Sometimes life is what happens when you aren't looking. I prefer to be looking. I don't want to live my life unconsciously. It is too precious to throw away.

When I was a kid in school, I couldn't wait for time to go by. Now I try to make time go as slow as possible. I want each moment to take an hour to go by like it did then. I have probably lived 2/3's of my life and I have worked hard to be aware of the moments as they have passed. Now I work even harder.

Each breath is an incredible gift that we borrow and have to give back. Something that is so simple yet so difficult to understand. The more we are aware of each one, the slower life goes by and the richer each day is. It fills the heart.

I Saw My Heart

I saw my heart
It launched joy and peace to the world
It blew kisses to small children and dogs
It danced in the wind as the leaves swirled by
It sang the song of joy that plays deep within
It felt the sorrow of love that was lost
It embraced the Grace that comes with each breath
It holds the Mother Earth tightly and loves it deeply

Thank God it's Saturday

Thank God it's Saturday, thank God it's any day and we are alive. I have a friend that I tell that even if we are suffering, it is incredible to be alive. It is. Each breath is an amazing gift that we/I so often don't notice. Yet nothing we do has any worth without it. It is the most precious gift. Without it, nothing has value as we are not here.

Being aware of the breath, slows time down and makes us more appreciative of the world and what a magical place it is. Take the time to watch your breath at least once.

There Was a Man

There was a man who would speak to God
He was a humble man
His desire was only to serve God
The infinite
He sought no glory
No recognition
No fame
Only that moment of connection where he was one
Only that connection where he knew that God was
He heard no voice
Saw no burning bush
Parted no seas
It was simple
A small thing really
But just as great a miracle as any ever told
He took a breath
And there was God to behold

Where Has the Will Gone

Where has the will gone
The will to be free
The will to be
We accept so much
We don't fight
We fight the things we shouldn't
Like
Love
Compassion
Gratitude
Acceptance
Receiving
Care
Affection
Time to open our hearts
Stop fighting these gifts
Quit resisting love
Give compassion
Be grateful
Accept the things we cannot change
Receive with open arms
Care with all our hearts
Give and receive affection without strings
It would make this world
The world we crave

Wandering Soul

Where might you be off to my little wandering soul
The stars aren't too far
The moon is close
My heart is even closer
Might you wander there
I would love you
I would hold you
I would make you mine
But I would set you free
That's what true love does
It spreads the wings
It makes the heart soar
Travels happen to places unheard of
Joy is the great destination

The Vulnerability of the Heart

The vulnerability of the heart is well known to us all
We guard
Protect it all the time
We have learned this from the time we were born
We learn it at home
We learn it at school
You don't leave your heart open
Others will try to break it
It is an unspoken law
You do not open your heart
You do not be vulnerable
If you do leave it open
It will be beaten
You will be beaten
Time for us to stop this
Time for us to change this world
Take the chance
Show others your heart is strong
Yes you can be hurt
Yes you are afraid
But you are brave
You will take a chance
You will help with healing this world
When you show your heart
An amazing thing will happen
Your heart gets stronger
The blows don't hit home
When they do
You love the one that threw it

And move on
It's worth the chance
For love
For freedom
For you
For the world

Nothing Is Easier

Nothing is easier than breathing. Nothing. We don't have to do anything and it happens. It's magic. One day that magic will stop. One day that breath will go out and not return. It is time to pay attention, to be aware of the gift each breath is.

I have been around people getting ready to die. You learn how precious a breath is.

Acknowledgements

Thank you:

Chandler Bolt for inspiring me to believe I could publish a book and giving me the tools to do it.

Tom Corson-Knowles for your YouTube videos on how to format and publish a book.

Hal Elrod for "The Miracle Morning". You helped me change my thinking patterns in a wonderful way.

My favorite sister Deb MacLeod for editing and giving sisterly love, support and riding in a sled backwards.

Azlan MacLeod for the cover layout

Dan MacLeod for the cover design idea

Midtown Writers Group for all your support and love and being such awesome writers. You inspire me every week.

Lorenzo at A la Salsa restaurant for allowing your space to be used for 10 years to write then read every Saturday. Selena and the rest of the staff as well for looking after us during that time.

Jeanne Bain for inspiring me to write, loving me, getting me, being your weird self, loving your people, miraculously getting well, staying on the planet and just being awesome.

Joe MacLeod, my father, for being a poet and somehow passing that on without ever sharing your poetry with me. Tag, you're it.

Mary Virginia Swicord MacLeod, my mom, for being my biggest fan. For telling me stories as a child. For being your wonderful self. For seeing and knowing me.

Ellen Finholt MacLeod you lovely being. I am amazed at what you have become. Angelic does not describe it. Being your secretary taught me to write. Sharing your struggle to live made me a writer. I miss you being on the planet, but look at what you made me do.

Last things

If you liked this book, please leave me feedback

Thank you for reading

I don't know exactly how to say this, but it is what I try to convey in my poetry. You know those moments, the ones that you wish you could sustain. Like the way you feel when you see a beautiful sunset or sunrise. The moment you see a wild animal being free and you feel that freedom, that connection they have. Or being by the ocean, a river or stream and a peacefulness engulfs you. The beauty is almost overwhelming in those moments. Those are the moments we feel the connection to our deepest self and to that thing that sustains us. This is what my teacher Prem Rawat taught me how to find and connect to every day many years ago. He showed me the way to focus inside and touch that place whenever and wherever I want.

As I have gotten older and learned to sustain it, it really has become available all the time if I choose and remember. I have learned to focus on something other than my thoughts and connect to something more beautiful than I could have imagined. So I thought I would invite you to check it out for yourselves.
Peace, tranquility and joy are so possible.

www.timelesstoday.com
www.theypi.net
www.wopg.org

www.ingramcontent.com/pod-product-compliance
Lightning Source LLC
Chambersburg PA
CBHW071754080526
44588CB00013B/2235